CALUMET CITY PUBLIC LIBRARY

3 1613 00503 4163

 **W9-BYG-331**

J
796.9
LAU

Ret 27.00 9-16

SNOWBOARDING

BY KARA L. LAUGHLIN

CALUMET CITY PUBLIC LIBRARY

Published by The Child's World®
1980 Lookout Drive • Mankato, MN 56003-1705
800-599-READ • www.childsworld.com

ACKNOWLEDGMENTS
The Child's World®: Mary Swensen, Publishing Director
The Design Lab: Design
Heidi Hogg: Editing
Sarah M. Miller: Editing

PHOTO CREDITS
© Action Photos/Shutterstock.com: 16; Becky Wass/Shutterstock.com: 19; Dmitry Naumov/Shutterstock.com: 10; Ipatov/Shutterstock.com: cover, 1, 15; Ksana_uk/Shutterstock.com: 13; Lopolo/Shutterstock.com: 7; Marcel Jancovic/Shutterstock.com: 9; NatalieJean/Shutterstock.com: 20; Trofimov Denis/Shutterstock.com: 4; Yarygin/Shutterstock.com: 2-3

COPYRIGHT © 2017 by The Child's World®
All rights reserved. No part of this book may be reproduced or utilized in any form or by any means without written permission from the publisher.

ISBN: 9781503807792
LCCN: 2015958214

Printed in the United States of America
Mankato, MN
June, 2016
PA02300

TABLE OF CONTENTS

Let's Ride!

There is fresh **powder** on the hills. Let's **ride**! It is time to go snowboarding.

Fast Fact!

Snowboarding started in the 1960s. It is a combination of skateboarding, sledding, surfing, and skiing.

Equipment

Since snowboarding is done in snow, you will need warm clothes. A coat, snowpants, and gloves are important.

Snowboarding can be dangerous. You will need a helmet. Goggles protect your eyes. Lastly, you will need boots and a snowboard.

Fast Fact!
Snowboarding used to be called "snurfing."
The word was a blend of "snow" and "surfing."

The Board

A snowboard curls up at the ends. The front of the board is the **nose**. The back area is the **tail**.

A snowboard's long sides come in at the **waist**. Metal **edges** grip the snow.

Fast Fact!
There are more than 8 million snowboarders just in North America.

9

10

The Bindings

Bindings keep your boots in place. Some snowboards have strap-in bindings. Others have step-in bindings. Make sure everything fits snugly. Then off you go!

Fast Fact!
Most bindings have the left foot in front. Bindings with the right foot in front are called "goofy."

Getting Up the Slope

You will need to get to the top of the **slope**. A **ski lift** will take you there. Some lifts carry people high above the snow. Others tow people from the ground. But all ski lifts have the same job—they get people up the slope.

Fast Fact!
Some people call ski lifts "chairlifts." That is because the lift is often shaped like a chair or bench.

3 1613 00503 4163

CALUMET CITY PUBLIC LIBRARY

13

Carving Turns

Time to go down the slope! Snowboarders make a zigzag path as they ride. A boarder **carves** a turn by leaning into an edge. This is also how a snowboarder stops.

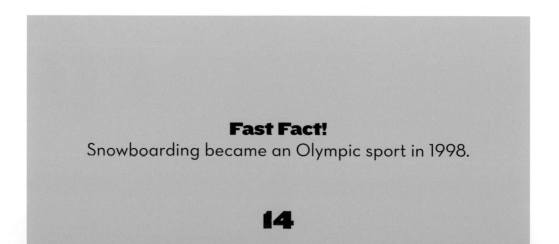

Fast Fact!
Snowboarding became an Olympic sport in 1998.

Freestyle Parks

Some snowboarders like to ride in **freestyle parks**. These parks are places to try out tricks. There are rails to slide on. There are all kinds of ramps for jumps and tricks.

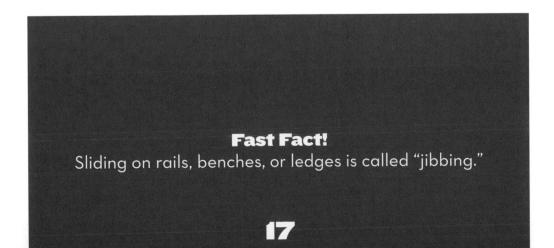

Fast Fact!
Sliding on rails, benches, or ledges is called "jibbing."

Tricks

An **ollie** is a good first trick. It is a little hop that takes the board off the ground. If they get enough **air**, riders can add **grabs**, spins, and turns.

Fast Fact!
Shawn White is a famous snowboarder. His nickname is "The Flying Tomato" because of his red hair.

Some snowboarders compete for style. Others race. Some like **half-pipe** runs. Others like to freestyle.

No matter what they are doing, all snowboarders agree—if you are having fun, you win!

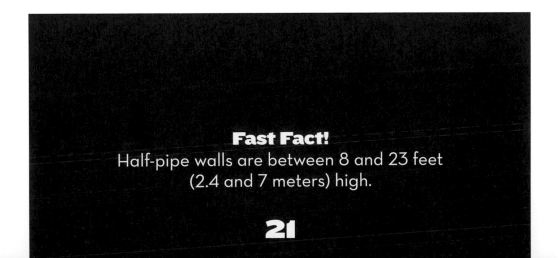

Fast Fact!
Half-pipe walls are between 8 and 23 feet
(2.4 and 7 meters) high.

Glossary

air (AYR): A lot of space between the snowboard and the ground. A jump that is very high gets a lot of air.

bindings (BYND-ingz): The parts that hold the boot onto the snowboard are called bindings.

carve (CARV): When riders carve, they use edges to turn.

edges (EDJ-ez): Edges are the thin pieces of metal along the sides of snowboards.

freestyle parks (FREE-styl PARKS): Slopes for freestyle snowboarders to do tricks are called freestyle parks.

grabs (GRABZ): Grabs are tricks in which the snowboarder grasps part of the board while in the air.

half-pipe (HAF-pipe): A half-pipe is a large, snow-covered area shaped like the bottom half of a tube.

nose (NOHZ): The front part of a snowboard is called the nose.

ollie (AHL-ee): A basic snowboard trick where the rider leans into the back leg to flex the board. Then he pops up and makes the board hop.

powder (POW-der): Powder is light, fluffy snow with no ice chunks.

ride (RIDE): To ride is to go down a slope on a snowboard.

ski lift (SKEE LIFT): A machine that takes snowboarders up a mountain is called a ski lift.

slope (SLOHP): A slope is a trail down a mountain for skis and snowboards.

tail (TAYL): The back part of a snowboard is called the tail.

waist (WAYST): The waist is the spot in the middle of the snowboard where the sides curve in.

To Learn More

In the Library

Fitzpatrick, Jim. *Snowboarding*. Ann
Arbor, MI: Cherry Lake, 2009.

Kleh, Cindy. *Being a Snowboarder*.
Minneapolis, MN: Lerner, 2013.

Laine, Carolee. *Inventing the Snowboard*.
Mankato, MN: The Child's World, 2016.

On the Web

Visit our Web site for links about snowboarding:
childsworld.com/links

Note to Parents, Teachers, and Librarians: We routinely verify
our Web links to make sure they are safe and active sites.
So encourage your readers to check them out!

Index

About the Author

Kara L. Laughlin is an artist and writer who lives in Virginia with her husband, three kids, two guinea pigs, and a dog. She is the author of two dozen nonfiction books for kids.